Your Best Life

A Manifestation Guidebook to Help You Live an Abundant Life

Elizabeth A. Till

BALBOA.
PRESS

A DIVISION OF HAY HOUSE

Balboa Press books may be ordered through booksellers or by contacting:

Balboa Press
A Division of Hay House
1663 Liberty Drive
Bloomington, IN 47403
www.balboapress.com
1 (877) 407-4847

ISBN: 978-1-9822-0317-7 (sc)
ISBN: 978-1-9822-0323-8 (e)

Library of Congress Control Number: 2019903686

Print information available on the last page.

Balboa Press rev. date: 03/26/2019

Your Best Life:
A Manifestation Guidebook
to Help You Live an
Abundant Life

I welcome you to this book, which is designed to awaken the powerful, life-changing potential that is already within you. It introduces a practical and transformative technique for creating the life you desire. The process is simple and fun to do, while profound in its results. My development and use of this practice aligned me with my highest potential. Thereby, I created the life I always wanted. I shared this method with family, friends, and clients who encouraged me to publish and share it with an even broader audience. With the help of my beloved daughter, who has been my inspiration, I present this guidebook to you. My blessings are imprinted on every page: mentally, physically, emotionally, and spiritually. Now it is up to you to dive in, put its wisdom to use, and utilize your innate powers to create a more joyful life.

Our journey begins with an understanding of what I refer to as the universal law of manifestation. When we manifest, we bring that which we imagine into physical reality. It may surprise you to discover that you are manifesting the people, the things, and the situations in your life. Every day you are internally and externally speaking thoughts to yourself. What you may not realize is that each of these thoughts carries a specific vibration into the universe. Whether these vibrational thoughts are negative or positive does not matter. They draw circumstances to you that perfectly match your thought patterns. In other words, you get exactly what you focus on.

Vibrations are not something the average individual is able to see, yet we are able to experience them through our emotions. If you can think of these emotions as being positive or negative, you can better understand vibrational frequency. When you are in a lower vibration, you don't feel good. You are restricting joy and limiting your potential. Likewise, when you feel good, joyful, and blessed, you are in a higher vibration and your emotional state is soaring. Being observant of your feelings is essential in creating the life you desire. The pages of this workbook enable you to experience and radiate unconditional love and appreciation. It assists you in understanding that positive, conscious awareness is the key component in obtaining and maintaining a happier, healthier you.

You may tend to think of your positive experiences as sheer luck and your unpleasant experiences as random misfortune or the fault of someone else. However those in the habit of forming benevolent thoughts attract more favorable experiences. In turn, negative thinkers habitually create and trap themselves in spirals of detrimental experiences without realizing they are the source of their own troubles. It is true; attitude is everything. Retraining our thoughts to broadcast positive vibrations is beneficial to you and to everyone you encounter. The Universe (also known as God, Spirit, Life, Source, Divine, or whatever name you prefer) is constantly mirroring your focused attention.

Your thought patterns call the universal law of manifestation into action and bring forth physical reality. This means that the first step in creating the life you want is to pay close attention to your thoughts. It is easy to respond to an experience without conscious awareness. For example, if your car battery is dead you may reason, "Just my luck. Bad things always happen to me," and curse the car and the situation. If you can catch yourself in this negative pattern, you can choose to rewrite the story. Instead, you may affirm, "My car is reliable. I take good care of it as it takes good care of me." Your thoughts, which represent your focus, are creating your present and future reality. These thought patterns can even be passed on to future generations of children. Can you imagine the gift of breaking your negative patterns before your children inherit them? Know that you have the power to break these chains.

I know this simple explanation of truth can empower you to envision and create a better life for yourself. You are about to engage in a hands-on practice where manifestation is made easy and fun. Throughout my years as a parent and an educator, I made the mundane and difficult concepts easier to learn through techniques that created flare and interest. This is the foundation for this workbook. It inspires you to shift your attitude into joy and appreciation almost instantly. It facilitates a profound sense of contentment that aligns you with the creative life force. Within this alignment springs forth your heart's desire in physical form. This is the most sought-after secret of life, and it is yours to enjoy.

Wherever you are on this journey, I assure you that everything is as it should be. Trust that you have Divine help. Know that you have personal abilities beyond limited thinking that await your claim. Remember this, dear friend; manifesting a better life is rewarding and truly empowering.

My Story

You may be wondering how I know that the law of manifestation is always working. I know this because I experienced the power of it firsthand. I once perceived myself as a victim. I believed that life was happening to me instead of the other way around. I seemed to draw varying degrees of abuse into my life from different individuals. I had no clue that I had attracted these people, nor that I had the power to change this pattern. It took deep introspection on my part to discover that my self-destructive thoughts originated at birth and solidified during my childhood.

Unfortunately, my mother almost died during my delivery, and we were immediately separated from one another. Instead of celebrating my newborn arrival, I was surrounded by panic and fear from everyone in the delivery room. We remained in the hospital for over a month, and during this time, I received little touch or nurturing from her. My mother was on the brink of death, fighting for her own life. After five and a half weeks of hospitalization, we were finally able to go home on Christmas Day. I was being passed around and held by my brother and two sisters when suddenly, I stopped breathing. Knowing CPR, my father resuscitated me before medical help arrived, and I was whisked back to the hospital.

Undoubtedly, this took a tremendous toll on my mother's already weakened condition.

Years later, I sought to identify and make sense of several inappropriate life choices I had made. I was an effective and loving teacher and had many friends. Yet, I did not understand why my most intimate relationships were painful and doomed to fail. With determination to understand myself, I turned to the source of my insecurities. I realized there was little or no bonding between my mother and me during this critical time in our lives. I believe my mother looked upon me as a source of fear, distrust, and resentment on a subconscious level. Misperceptions shadowed my reality, which left me feeling unworthy of true happiness. Over time I began to appreciate and understand that this was a treasure my mother gifted me with. The confusion I felt for so many years created separation deep within my soul. This was the gem that motivated me to heal my life. And it contributed to a promise and commitment I made to be fearless and follow my joy. This truth shaped my very first manifestation worksheet, which prompted me to immediately name it, *My Best Life*.

Certainly, my mother's and my difficult experience developed the belief in me that I was unworthy of love, and my thoughts continued to attract abuse long into adulthood. Now it is obvious to me that my perceived helplessness was all that I could imagine. Amid yet another offensive connection, I discovered that I was pregnant. I felt overwhelming joy at the prospect of becoming a mother, yet I knew something had to shift in my life. I craved to give and receive unconditional love. I desired to immerse myself in motherhood and the joy of life that had eluded me for so long.

Then the blessed "a-ha" moment came. While my newborn daughter slept soundly in my arms, I stood in front of a pet store window and peered at a little gray mouse in a clear plastic ball. I remember how sad and desperate that scene appeared to me. I witnessed a frantic and unaware creature rolling round and around the display case while moving as fast as his tiny legs would carry him. He was destined to go nowhere and did not even know it. Suddenly, I realized that mouse was me. I had repeated the same scenario over and over and over again just like this dismal, unaware little soul. Why had I felt powerless? Tears streamed down my face as I helplessly looked at my beautiful baby. At that very moment, I vowed to make changes. I was determined to take charge of my life. Somehow, I knew I must break the chains of bondage that had kept me small, which would claim this angel in my arms as well. (In retrospect, I realize I did not love myself enough to make the necessary changes on my own.) Thankfully, the love I felt for my child was overwhelming. She was the one who catapulted me onto the path of inner healing and self-discovery.

I became an avid reader of self-help books, took biblical and energetic healing classes, listened to inspirational speakers, and learned to tune into my own intuition. I gradually recognized my focus was misguided, and the problems I manifested were one and the same. I searched through my past for the source of these hurtful patterns, until I realized that I no longer needed to diminish who I was. When I decidedly changed my thought patterns to the present, the past was healed. I shifted defeatist thoughts to uplifting ones. I began to discern who I was and what was truly in my best interest. My once-perceived victimhood turned into a deep understanding, and my life patterns eventually became precious gifts. Everything happened as it was supposed to happen. I rose from the ashes like the proverbial phoenix and claimed my truth. Step by step, I healed my broken life with burning determination and inner fortitude.

After years of introspection and deep healing work, I fell in love with me: purely, simply, and with gusto. I began living and thinking in a way that brought positive experiences to me. Subsequently, I developed the following method of manifestation which I coined *Your Best Life*, and I lovingly present it to you. The healing technique you are about to experience is meant to lead you into a joyful state of being. In turn, it will activate positive thoughts, feelings, and expressions in you. As you go through the pages of this guidebook (although it could also be called a play book), allow yourself to feel the power of positive thoughts through your own glorious desires. Expect miracles awaiting your claim, always be in gratitude, and enjoy your new abundant life.

With love ... create your joy,
Elizabeth

Your Best Life Directions

1. Close your eyes and take several deep breaths, inhaling and exhaling through the nose if possible. Do not hurry the process. Breathwork is the most powerful way to align yourself with creative energy. You will become balanced in body and mind.

2. Allow your heart's desire to rise in your awareness. Choose only one desire per work page and focus on it completely. This desire can be symbolized in a word, a phrase, or a complete sentence. Write it within the heart, which is the center of your worksheet. This becomes the theme for the entire expression. Make sure it is stated as an affirmation in the present tense (e.g., instead of, "I will not eat unhealthy food" write, "I lovingly nourish and support my wonderful body"). This is important because the universe does not recognize negatives, and you would be calling in that which you want to avoid. (See my three completed *Your Best Life* samples starting on page 14-19).

3. I want you to feel your honest emotions, whether these are negative or positive. This honesty will be the fuel that raises your vibrations. Even if you are overcome by anger in the moment, it is necessary to use this feeling in a productive way. All emotions will transform into powerful joy as you dive into the process with intent and awareness. Positive emotion is required to obtain what you truly desire. Remember that the potent energy of your emotional expression is the mechanism that produces the universal law of manifestation. The universe adores and responds to passion.

   I once manifested the sale of my home as I intentionally changed negative emotions into positive ones. Initially, I was angry as I began working on my worksheet. Yet the hostility lifted as my thoughts focused on my theme and what I truly wanted. I turned my anger into genuine joy and appreciation as I imagined the perfect, loving, wonderful couple purchasing my home at a fair price. To my surprise, gracious buyers agreed to everything I envisioned, which included the price to the penny. I discovered that transformed anger generated the momentum I needed to manifest what I wanted. It became a powerful understanding.

The more you include your five senses in this process, the more promising the outcome. Focus on creating sensations and feelings that involve sight, smell, sound, touch, and taste. With intention, you generate an atmosphere that aligns with your deepest desires. These simple actions shift something within you. It is your truth. You experience it in the moment. Miraculously, it manifests into physical reality. You can choose anything that increases your sensitivities. Which ones make you feel good?

Here are a few suggestions that I have used: soothing music, scented candles, essential oils rubbed into your skin, things of beauty such as flowers, or other cherished items, chocolates that beg consumption, or dress in your favorite outfit with hair in place.

Sadness is a different type of energy that may require extra attention. I suggest you take action to raise your vibration before doing the writing process or focusing on your sensitivities. With clear intention choose to sing, dance, read a happy poem or short story, give love to a pet, visualize that you are holding a new-born, do yoga, exercise, or walk in nature. Raise your vibration. Feel better. Next, include any of the above ideas, breathe, and begin *Your Best Life* worksheet.

4. Locate the inner portion of the worksheet. Fill in all spaces with words, statements, sentences, and symbols of adoration. These create happiness within your soul. The Universe adores passion. Thus, become lost within the heart of your creation. Give yourself permission to become animated and full of love, life, and fun-filled expression. The more you feel your desire is, the more powerful you become. Do not hold back.

5. Every statement needs to reflect intentional ownership of your creative power. The more you feel your desire is and has already manifested, the more powerful you become. Thus, there is no need to ask for anything. See it. Feel it. Breathe it. Know it is yours, now. Claim your truth with bold confidence.

6. Deep appreciation for what is becomes extremely important to the process. Give thanks and weave symbols of joy into your expression (e.g., hearts, stars, flowers). Words of gratitude may be added alongside the illustrations (see samples on page 17).

7. Color the symbols, the lines, and the heartbeat in the middle section of the letter. Choose to color the illustrations, outline them, or leave them black and white. Your masterpiece is your masterpiece. Become lost in the heart of *Your Best Life* worksheet.

8. Place your finished work of genius in a sacred place, such as an altar. You may prefer to place it on your mirror or in a convenient location where you can reread it. Do one or more letters using the same theme if you wish.

9. Do not agonize about the outcome or wonder how or when your desire will manifest. Let it go and let God. Some things come quickly while other things take more time and may need repetition. Use your own good judgement. Know that it already is, and all is well.

Your Best Life
3 Sample Pages

Sample 1

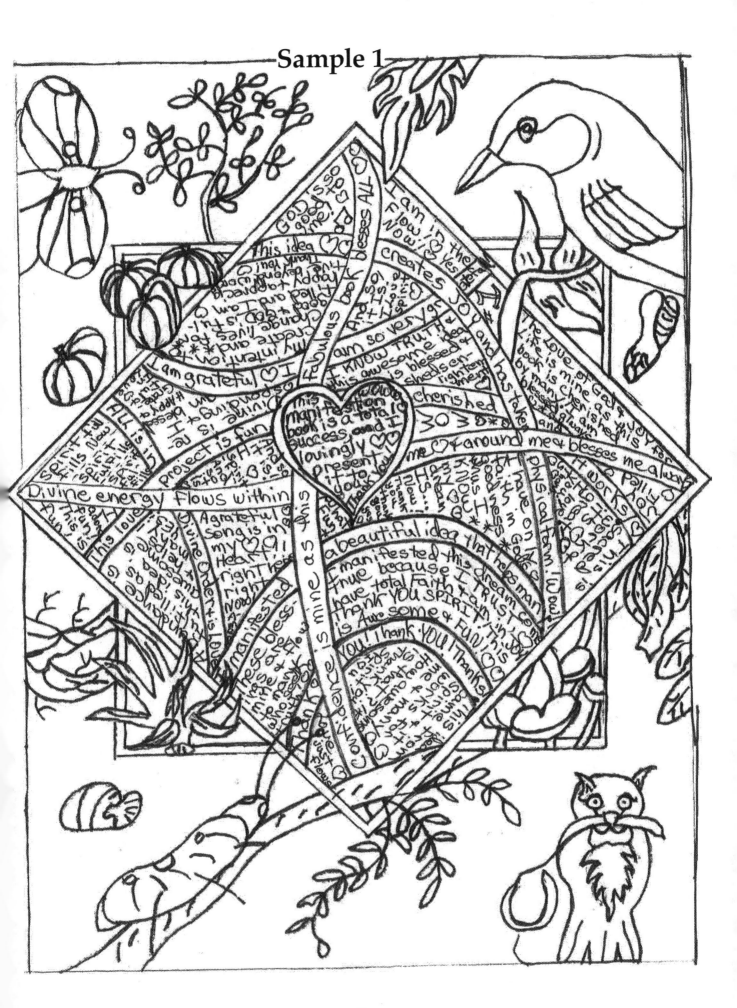

Positive Word List

Abundance	Compassion	Fun	Leisure	Rejoice
Accept	Connection	Gentle	Life	Release
Adventure	Content	Gifts	Light	River of Life
Amazed	Create	God	Love	Sacred
Amen	Creativity	Grateful	Lovingly	Safe
Appreciation	Delight	Gratitude	Miracle	Self-realize
Awaken	Desire	Grow	New	Serenity
Aware	Divine Guidance	Hallelujah	Now	Simplicity
Authentic	Divine Order	Harmony	Oneness	Smile
Awesome	Divine Path	Healed	Open	Success
Belong	Eager	Honesty	Overflowing	Support
Beautiful	Easy	Honor	Overjoyed	Surrender
Beauty	Ecstatic	Humor	Passion	Synchronicity
Blessed	Efficiency	Ideas	Patience	Tenderness
Blessing	Energy	Inner child	Peace	Thanks
Bliss	Enlightenment	Integrity	Peaceful	Thrilled
Blissful	Excited	Inspiration	Perfect	Transform
Blossom	Expression	Integrate	Playful	Trust
Celebrate	Extend	Interesting	Pleasing	Truth
Cheerful	Faith	Joy	Pleasure	Whole
Cherish	Fantastic	Joy-filled	Powerful	Wisdom
Clarity	Flexible	Journey	Precious	Wise
Closure	Focus	Jubilant	Present	Wonderment
Communion	Free	Know	Prosperity	Wow
Community	Freedom	Knowingness	Purpose	Yes

Positive Phrases

Ability to manifest
Already is
Always supported
Angel's touch
Awareness is
Awareness of mind
Best ... ever
Cherished always
Chosen family
Community arises
Compassion of heart
Decision of heart
Deliberate joy
Desired focus
Divine Order is
Expanding heart
Express easily
Family blesses
Freedom now
Freely given
Fun-filled journey
God's blessings
Grateful for
Happy me
Happy days
Healing now
Heavenly bliss
Humor heals

Joy-filled relationship
Joyful thoughts
Laughter heals
Loving service
Making memories
Matter of Faith
Miracles manifest
Oh yes
Open heart
Playful expression
Plunging in
Plenty of money
Present state
Sense of knowing
Shifted thinking
Sacred alignment
Silly and free
So joyful
Soul connection
Spirit lifts
Stepping into
Teaches patience
Total faith
Totally successful
Truly beautiful
Winning in
Wonderful changes
Wonderful place

Positive Statements

Change is truly exhilarating. I celebrate and allow a new me. Thank you, God.

Discovering my voice allows me to sing my own praises. I am (dynamic, thrilled).

Divine energy surrounds and moves me toward my beautiful (life, partner, desire).

Growth is who I am. Change is with grace and ease. I am (excited, open, creative).

I am a fabulous (adventurer, writer, healer, risk-taker, mother, friend), and it shows.

I am a good listener and great friend. I attract others easily. All is well.

I am blessed with this perfect (mate, job, child, parent). I appreciate (him/her, it).

I am healthy and whole. My body, mind, and spirit are well. Thank you. And it is.

I am part of the river of life. It carries me, always. Miracles are truly mine.

I am peaceful within my soul. I allow this contentment here and now. Amen.

I am (wise, awesome, open) to change. Everything is in divine order. All is perfect

I am wonderment personified, and I know it. Thank you, spirit. Halleluiah.

I am (worthy, healthy, courageous, wonderful, talented) and oh so beautiful.

I communicate easily and effectively. I am heard. It feels so refreshing.

I completely let go and let God. Thank you, spirit. Thank you. Thank you. And it is.

I celebrate my new (position, partner, challenge, truth). Life is oh so good. Yes.

I embrace (challenge you are facing) with grace and ease. I know all is well.

I give and receive with love. Being in service feels heavenly. I am so grateful.

I love me, and it glows. I take great care of my amazing body. Kisses to me. Yes.

I know I am blessed now. I am in the flow. Life is fabulously wonderful.

I (know, trust, surrender, allow). All is well. All is really (really) well. Joy is mine.

I learn, listen, and grow. I embrace (change life experiences). Courageous me.

It feels marvelous to be in love. I love (myself, person, God). I appreciate us.

Joyfully, I embrace (challenge). My wisdom, and courage, are empowering.

(Love, patience, strength, tenderness, understanding) are exactly who I am.

Manifestation is fun and empowering beyond belief. I am appreciative. Wow.

My positive thoughts, trust, and attitude empower me. I manifest easily.

My potential is aligned with God. We are loveable, deserving, and beautiful.
My wise inner child and I are one. We are loveable, deserving, and beautiful.
My wonderful (job, relationship, life, goal) is growing me beyond belief. Wow.
My wonderful relationship with (person, boss, child) is a gift. Divine order is now.
(Name person) and I are one. We respect and cherish each other. It is magical.
(Name person in conflict) blesses me. We treasure our relationship and growth.
Self-care is everything. I know what is in my best interest. I take great care of me.
Thank you, God (or preferred name). Thank you. Thank you. I appreciate you.
(Your challenge) is a great opportunity for enlightenment. All is well.
(Your desire) feels (great, fabulous, special, wonderful). Miracles are mine, now.

Bring to Life Your
Deepest Desires

About the Author

Elizabeth Till is an intuitive healer and angel communicator who lives in the mountains near Asheville, North Carolina. Having had a near death experience as a baby opened Elizabeth's connection to Source. This experience enabled her to easily access the unseen, deeper realms of reality. However, she did not understand her innate, intuitive ability until the birth of her daughter, Christa. This life-changing event ignited the desire to heal her life.

A boating accident, a series of health problems, and an acute sensitivity to pharmaceuticals, led Elizabeth to turn to alternative methods of healing. She began studying proper nutrition, medicinal herbs, natural remedies, and other alternative treatment modalities. Her travels to sacred sites in Southern France initiated her into ancient wisdom. This led her to six years of research and discovery into the secret life of Mary Magdalene. Immersion in these ancient traditions inspired her to learn the art of powerful energy healing and blessing work. Thirty years of intuitive readings, clearing and healing work for others followed.

Elizabeth wrote *Your Best Life,* with the intention of making manifestation simple and easy for anyone to do. This sacred tool can help bring what we truly want into our lives in a fun and uplifting way. It is a gift of love. It is her hope that everyone who reads it will discover the joy and happiness that is their human birthright.

You may wish to communicate with Elizabeth concerning her guidebook or schedule an angel reading with her, You can do this through her website at .,,,, or email her at HYPERLINK "mailto:angelcall2mmy@gmail.com" angelcall2mmy@ gmail.com.

Printed in the United States
By Bookmasters